Experience God's Power

Revelation

New Community Bible Study Series

JOHN ORTBERG

WITH KEVIN **&** SHERRY HARNEY

New Community
KNOWING. LOVING. SERVING. CELEBRATING.

Experience
God's Power

REVELATION

GRAND RAPIDS, MICHIGAN 49530

ZONDERVAN™

Revelation: Experience God's Power
Copyright © 2002 by the Willow Creek Association

Requests for information should be addressed to:

Zondervan, *Grand Rapids, Michigan 49530*

ISBN: 0-310-22882-4

Interior design by Sherri Hoffman

Printed in the United States of America

02 03 04 05 06 07 /❖ CH/ 10 9 8 7 6 5 4 3 2 1

CONTENTS

God has created us for community. This need is built into the very fiber of our being, the DNA of our spirit. As Christians, our deepest desire is to see the truth of God's Word as it influences our relationship with others. We long for a dynamic encounter with God's Word, intimate closeness with His people, and radical transformation of our lives. But how can we accomplish those three difficult tasks?

The New Community Bible Study Series creates a place for all of this to happen. In-depth Bible study, community-building opportunities, and life-changing applications are all built into every session of this small group study guide.

How to Build Community

How do we build a strong, healthy Christian community? The whole concept for this study grows out of a fundamental understanding of Christian community that is dynamic and transformational. We believe that Christians don't simply gather to exchange doctrinal affirmations. Rather, believers are called by God to get into each other's lives. We are family, for better or for worse, and we need to connect with each other.

Community is not built through sitting in the same building and singing the same songs. It is forged in the fires of life. When we know each other deeply—the good, the bad, and the ugly—community is experienced. Community grows when we learn to rejoice with one another, celebrating life. Roots grow deep when we know we are loved by others and are free to extend love to them as well. Finally, community deepens and is built when we commit to serve each other and let others serve us. This process of doing ministry and humbly receiving the ministry of others is critical for healthy community life.

Build Community Through Knowing and Being Known

We all long to know others deeply and to be fully known by them. Although we might run from this level of intimacy at times, we all want to have people in our lives who trust us enough to disclose the deep and tender parts of themselves. In turn, we want to reveal some of our feelings, expressing them freely to people we trust.

The first section of each of these six studies creates a place for deep knowing and being known. Through serious reflection on the truth of Scripture, you will be invited to communicate parts of your heart and life with your small group members. You might even discover yourself opening parts of your heart that you have thus far kept hidden. The Bible study and discussion questions do not encourage surface conversation. The only way to go deep in knowing others and being known by them is to dig deep, and this takes some work. Knowing others also takes trust—that you will honor each other and respect each other's confidences.

Build Community Through Celebrating and Being Celebrated

If you have not had a good blush recently, read a short book in the Bible called Song of Songs. It's a record of a bride and groom writing poetic and romantic love letters to each other. They are freely celebrating every conceivable aspect of each other's personality, character, and physical appearance. At one point the groom says, "You have made my heart beat fast with a single glance from your eyes." Song of Songs is a reckless celebration of life, love, and all that is good.

We need to recapture the joy and freedom of celebration. In every session of this study, your group will commit to celebrate together. Although there are many ways to express joy, we will let our expression of celebration come through prayer. In each session you will take time to come before the God of joy and celebrate who He is and what He is doing. You will also have opportunity to celebrate what God is doing in your life and the lives of those who are a part of your small group. You will become a community of affirmation, celebration, and joy through your prayer time together.

You will need to be sensitive during this time of prayer together. Not everyone feels comfortable praying with a group of people. Be aware that each person is starting at a different place in their freedom to pray in a group, so be patient. Seek to promote a warm and welcoming atmosphere where each person can stretch a little and learn what it means to be a community that celebrates with God in the center.

Build Community Through Loving and Being Loved

Unless we are exchanging deeply committed levels of love with a few people, we will die slowly on the inside. This is precisely why so many people feel almost nothing at all. If we don't learn to exchange love with family and friends, we will eventually grow numb and no longer believe love is even a possibility. This is not God's plan. He hungers for us to be loved and to give love to others. As a matter of fact, He wants this for us even more than we want it for ourselves.

Every session in this study will address the area of loving and being loved. You will be challenged, in your personal life and as a small group, to be intentional and consistent about building love relationships. You will get practical tools and be encouraged to set measurable goals for giving and receiving love.

Build Community Through Serving and Being Served

Community is about serving and humbly allowing others to serve you. The single most stirring example of this is recorded in John 13, where Jesus takes the position of the lowest servant and washes the feet of His followers. He gives them a powerful example and then calls them to follow. Servanthood is at the very core of community. To sustain deep relationships over a long period of time, there must be humility and a willingness to serve each other.

At the close of each session will be a clear challenge to servanthood. As a group, and as individual followers of Christ, you will discover that community is built through serving others. You will also find that your own small group members will grow in their ability to extend service to your life.

Bible Study Basics

To get the most out of this study, you will need to prepare and participate. Here are some guidelines to help you.

Preparing for the Study

1. If possible, even if you are not the leader, look over each session before you meet, read the Bible passages, and answer the questions. The more you are prepared, the more you will gain from the study.
2. Begin your preparation time with prayer. Ask God to help you understand the passage and apply it to your life.
3. A good modern translation, such as the New International Version, the New American Standard Bible, or the New Revised Standard Version, will give you the most help. Questions in this guide are based on the New International Version.
4. Read and reread the passages. You must know what the passage says before you can understand what it means and how it applies to you.
5. Write your answers in the spaces provided in the study guide. This will help you participate more fully in the discussion and will also help you personalize what you are learning.
6. Keep a Bible dictionary handy to look up unfamiliar words, names, or places.

Participating in the Study

1. Be willing to join in the discussion. The leader of the group will not be lecturing but will encourage people to discuss what he or she has learned in the passage. Plan to share what God has taught you during your preparation time.
2. Stick to the passages being studied. Base your answers on the verses being discussed rather than on outside authorities such as commentaries or your favorite author or speaker.

3. Try to be sensitive to the other members of the group. Listen attentively when they speak, and be affirming whenever you can. This will encourage more hesitant members of the group to participate.
4. Be careful not to dominate the discussion. By all means participate, but allow others to have equal time.
5. If you are a discussion leader or a participant who wants further insights, you will find additional comments in the Leader's Notes at the back of this book.

Revelation: Experience God's Power

When is the world going to end? In our day? In our lifetime? Who is the Antichrist? What is the mark of the beast? What will heaven be like? These and countless other questions are on the minds of followers of Christ around the world. The book of Revelation is the source of many of these questions. In fact, it would be fair to say that there is not another book of the Bible that is the subject of more curiosity, confusion, or speculation than the book of Revelation.

When it comes to the book of Revelation, people in the church tend to have two primary responses. Sadly, both of these responses are unhealthy. There are those who become obsessed with the book. They treat it like a prophetic jigsaw puzzle that will give them insider information if only they can put all the pieces together. They write up intricate time lines and diagrams that impressively chart out the last days and appear to offer answers to all of our questions.

Unfortunately, people who have this response often get diverted from their faith and become obsessed with speculation. When I was first getting started in church ministry back in the middle '80s, a man wrote a book giving eighty-eight reasons why the rapture would happen in 1988. He reasoned that, although the Bible teaches we *can't* know the day or the hour of Jesus' return, we *can* know the month and the year! But Jesus did not return in 1988. So what did this man do? Did he write an apology to the church and offer to give everyone their money back if they returned the book? No! He wrote a new book about why Jesus would return in 1989!

One author was so convinced that the return of Jesus was going to be in his lifetime that he wrote, "Desolating earthquakes, sweeping fires, distressing poverty, political profligacy, private bankruptcy, and widespread immorality abound in these last days, which obviously indicate that the Lord is returning immediately." These words were written by William Miller in 1843. He tragically disappointed tens of thousands of Christians who sat on hillsides looking upward and waiting for Jesus to return.

Another writer claims that the literal building blocks for the new temple in Israel have been constructed and numbered, and they are being stored in the basements of a major department store chain all over the United States until they can be shipped to Israel and used to build a new temple. All of this reminds me of a quote by the great Christian author G. K. Chesterton when he said, "Though St. John saw many strange monsters in his vision, he saw no creature so wild as one of his own commentators."

Remember the story about the boy who cried wolf? After awhile, nobody would listen to him. They had had enough of the false alarms! Then, when the wolf finally came, no one believed the boy when he cried out. I have serious concerns about those who are crying wolf by declaring to the world that they have figured out when Jesus will return. When seekers hear elaborate explanations about Jesus' second coming being given "in the name of Christ," and these theories go unfulfilled, we do serious damage to the evangelistic potential of future generations!

Jesus is very clear that none of us can know when He will return: "It is not for you to know the times or dates the Father has set by his own authority" (Acts 1:7). Jesus also says very clearly that He is coming back: "He who testifies to these things says, 'Yes, I am coming soon.' Amen. Come, Lord Jesus" (Revelation 22:20). What we *can't* know for sure is when He will return. Those who find themselves consumed with trying to figure out when Jesus will return can get caught up in a web that can damage not only their own faith but the faith of others as well.

A second response people may have to the book of Revelation is to avoid it altogether, either out of frustration or confusion. They say, "I can't make heads or tails of this book. It has bizarre images of strange creatures, beasts, blood, bowls of sulfur, people eating scrolls, bottomless pits, dragons, the four horses of the Apocalypse, war, pestilence, famine, and death!

It just does not seem like a very happy book." Because they can't understand what it is saying, they prefer to set it aside for others to grapple with. Sadly, these people are missing out on some powerful life lessons God wants to teach us through the book of Revelation.

Jesus does not want us to be engaged in wild speculation and date-setting for His return. Neither does He wish for us to be ignorant about any portion of the Bible, including Revelation. What Jesus wants is for us to be yielded to the Holy Spirit, to be His witnesses, to be about His work, to spread the gospel, to be spiritually awake, and to be increasingly alive to God's presence within us. Jesus wants His followers to be on the welcoming committee when He returns; He does not need anyone on the "when and where" committee. As a matter of fact, Jesus is clear that He wants His return to be a surprise!

As we walk through this study, we will strive to take Jesus at His word regarding the book of Revelation. We are not going to engage in foolish and unbiblical speculation; instead, we will seek a humble and biblical stance as we look closely at this powerful portion of Scripture. It is not our purpose to try to figure out what is reserved for God alone to know, but we will ask the Holy Spirit to mold and shape us into people who are ready to meet Jesus. If it is today or a thousand years from now, we will hear the call to be ready to meet our Lord.

Why Study the Book of Revelation?

REVELATION 1:1–8

We have all met her. She is so set in her ways that she will never try anything new. In her universe, there is only one flavor of ice cream: vanilla. It does not matter what the flavor of the month happens to be or what new concoction Ben & Jerry's has created. Vanilla it has been, vanilla it is now, vanilla it shall be forevermore!

We have all met him. We ask, "What do you want for Christmas?" and he gives the same old suggestions: Old Spice, new socks, a tie, slippers. How someone can go through a pair of slippers every year may be a mystery, but what is not a mystery is that his list this Christmas will be the same as last year, and the year before that, and the year before that.

Is there anything wrong with vanilla ice cream? No! Is putting the same items on a Christmas list year after year a crime? Of course not! But where is the adventure in life? Where is the willingness to be surprised by the taste of Double Fudgey Moose Track Ripple Supreme ice cream or to be willing to write "Surprise me!" on a Christmas list?

Try something new. Take a risk. Study a book of the Bible you have never dug into before. Live on the edge . . . you might find out you like it!

Making the Connection

1. Tell about a time you took a risk, tried something new, or made an effort to be adventuresome.

15

Knowing and Being Known

Read Revelation 1:1–8

2. The word "revelation" means "an act of unveiling or disclosure." What is unveiled about Jesus Christ in these opening verses?

3. Imagine you are a Christian living in the first century and you hear these eight verses read. What would a Christian understand about God, especially in verses 4–8?

4. How does this understanding of God give hope to the persecuted church?

Why Study Revelation? Because It's in the Bible

One of the marks of growth in fully devoted followers of Jesus is their commitment to study the whole counsel of God. Paul says to Timothy, "All Scripture is God-breathed and is useful for teaching, rebuking, correcting and training in righteousness" (2 Timothy 3:16). The apostle Paul is emphatic that we need all of the Bible's teaching—from Genesis to Revelation—if we are to grow up into mature believers. Many, however, prefer to study a few favorite or select portions of God's Word. Some people read only the Gospels, others favor the Psalms or Proverbs, and still others spend almost all of their time in Paul's letters. While study of each of these portions of the Bible is useful, Paul makes it clear that we will not get the whole picture and grow deep in maturity until we become students of the whole Bible.

Read 2 Timothy 3:14–17

5. How would you define each of the following words in relationship to the way God works in our lives through study of the Bible?

    - Teaching
    - Rebuking
    - Correcting
    - Training
    - Equipping

6. How have you experienced the God-breathed power of Scripture to bring transformation in your life through one of the five ways listed in this passage?

    Tell about one personal discipline God has called you to practice in your life when it comes to studying the Bible.

    How can your small group members pray for you and challenge you to grow deeper in your commitment to know and follow God's Word?

Why Study Revelation? It Contains Powerful Life Lessons

As we study the book of Revelation, we will be gripped by the powerful life lessons it has for us. First, we will come face-to-face with the reality of the battle of good and evil. We will come to realize that this battle is not just between nations, but it rages both in the heavenly realms and in our very hearts.

Second, we will be gripped by the reality of heaven and hell. John writes about the eternal condition of human souls with a power and style different from any other author in the Bible. In light of the staggering reality of the eternal destiny of all people in either heaven or hell, we will be moved to do the work of evangelism like never before.

And third, we will be confronted with the glorious triumph of Christ, even when we face tough times. John first wrote these words as a source of hope and encouragement to seven struggling churches in a time of intense persecution. Studying John's words to these churches will dramatically increase our confidence in the Lord.

Read Revelation 22:7, 12–21

7. In light of Jesus' words (Revelation 22:7) and John's words (Revelation 22:18–19), how would you respond to a follower of Christ who makes this statement: "The book of Revelation is too hard to understand, I don't think I want to bother reading it and try to figure out what it means for my life!"

8. Jesus paints a vivid picture of those who are inside and those who are outside His heavenly city (vv. 12–15). What are some of the contrasts you see between those who are inside and those who are outside of the kingdom of God?

9. What do you learn about the identity of Jesus Christ in verses 12–16. Why would these attributes of Jesus offer comfort for Christians in a time of persecution?

Why Study Revelation? It Carries the Promise of Blessing

Revelation is the only book in the New Testament that contains a clear and explicit promise of blessing for those who read it and follow what it teaches. Consider these words: "Blessed is the one who reads the words of this prophecy, and blessed are those who hear it and take to heart what is written in it, because the time is near" (Revelation 1:3) and "Behold, I am coming soon! Blessed is he who keeps the words of the prophecy in this book" (Revelation 22:7).

John says you are blessed (happy) if you read and follow the teaching of Revelation. The problem when we hear the word "blessed" is that we tend to think of financial gain, work going well, or our health being great. But the people to whom John was writing didn't feel lucky or blessed; they were being persecuted! Remember, John is writing from exile on a distant island, separated from the community he loves. Some of his followers were being tempted by false teachers, others were growing faint-hearted, some of them were apathetic, and many were tempted to throw in the towel when it came to their faith!

John says to them what he says to us today: If we read this book and keep working away at what it says, we will be blessed by God. Does this mean that all our circumstances will turn out exactly as we would want? No. But it does mean that we can learn to live and walk in the power and presence of Almighty God. And when Jesus comes again we will hear the words, "Well done, good and faithful servant."

10. Some would say, "I can experience blessedness and true happiness only when things are going well in my life." What do you think the apostle John would say to these people?

11. Describe a blessing you have experienced as you have studied and followed the teaching of the Bible.

Celebrating and Being Celebrated

We are promised that careful study of God's Word will bring transforming power in our lives. The apostle Paul (2 Timothy 3:16) is clear that God's Word has power to:

- Teach
- Rebuke
- Correct
- Train in righteousness

Take time as a small group to pray together, thanking God for how He has brought transformation in your life through the truth of His Word. Celebrate how He has taught, rebuked, corrected, and trained you through the Scriptures.

Loving and Being Loved

Jesus said, "Greater love has no one than this, that he lay down his life for his friends" (John 15:13). He went on to lay His life down to pay the price for sins and bring us into a restored relationship with the Father. As we study the book of Revelation it becomes clear that all people will spend eternity either in relationship with God in heaven or separated from God in hell. There is no middle ground.

Identify one practical act of love and care you can extend to a friend who is not a follower of Christ. Pray for the Holy Spirit to infuse your actions with His power so that this friend will begin to experience the love of God as you seek practical ways to serve and love him or her.

Serving and Being Served

In this session (Question 6) some of your small group members talked about their own personal disciplines when it comes to studying the Bible. They also talked about some of their goals in this area of their life. Talk as a group about how you can serve each other by keeping one another accountable to make time on a regular basis to study God's Word. Try to pair up so that each group member has one person praying for him and keeping him accountable to make personal study of the Bible a priority in his life over the coming month.

Understanding the Images and Language of Revelation

REVELATION 1:12–20

Friends of ours took a trip with their three-year-old daughter. While on the plane, the little girl experienced a great deal of pain because her ears were popping. She cried throughout most of the flight. The mom knew that chewing would relieve the pressure in her daughter's ears, so the next time the family traveled she brought along some animal crackers and told her daughter they would help with the pain in her ears while they were flying. Confused, but trusting the wisdom of her mother, the little girl took two animal crackers and proceeded to stick one in each of her ears.

This mother and daughter had what Bible scholars call a "hermeneutical problem." Somewhere between the speaker and the listener, communication broke down. Some kind of interpretation of the information was needed. The purpose of hermeneutics is to help us understand the reasons for the gap between the sender and receiver and to try to reduce this gap and minimize distortion in the communication process.

Correct interpretation is very important for those of us who seek to live under the authority of Scripture. We don't want to misread the Bible, nor do we want to be in a place where we have to always depend on someone else to tell us what the Bible says and means. If we do, we are always at the whim or mercy of whoever claims to have authority to teach the Bible.

There are rules involved in responsible biblical interpretation. It is not just a random process. If we want to understand the Bible with minimal distortion, we must learn to recognize and understand the figurative use of symbolism and metaphor throughout it. Very often people get in trouble because they get hung up on the pictures in the Bible and fail to realize the richness of the meaning behind them. For example, in the gospel of John, Jesus says, "I am the gate" (John 10:9). This does not mean Jesus is a literal gate with hinges and a handle. It is a metaphor—a way of expressing that His words, life, death, and resurrection are our gateway to God. Jesus is the way we enter into relationship with the Father. He is the only entrance into eternal life.

If we interpret the book of Revelation carefully and responsibly, it will begin to make sense and transform our lives. But if we try to plow through Revelation without doing good interpretive work, there will be a breakdown in communication—and we might just end up with animal crackers in our ears!

Making the Connection

1. Tell about a time when you experienced some kind of breakdown in communication where the words of the sender were different than the understanding of the receiver.

Knowing and Being Known

Read Revelation 1:12–20

Understanding Objects in the Book of Revelation

In this passage we see a vision of Jesus. Some of the objects in this vision communicate fairly easily and others might seem a bit harder to understand. One object we notice right away is that Jesus has a sharp, double-edged sword coming out of His mouth. This does not mean that when we see Jesus He will have a blade sticking out from His lips. We need to think about what a sword meant in John's day. The sword was the means of exercising authority and power. Whoever held the sword was in charge!

Even today, when we talk about our words and their power, we use imagery in a similar way. We have all heard the phrase "shooting off your mouth," which means that if we are not careful our words can fly like a stray bullet and cause great pain. We talk about "dodging verbal bullets," or someone "exploding in anger." The picture of the sword gives us a sense of Jesus' power and authority.

What John is saying to us with this powerful image is that in Jesus we have someone who has all the authority needed to back up what He says. This was true from the beginning of creation, when God spoke and everything came into existence. God could say to the sun "Rise," and it rose, because His words have absolute authority. And this is still true today.

2. What is one object or image in this passage that jumps out at you and how does it help you understand the person and character of Jesus? (Look at Daniel 7:9–10, 13 and 10:5–6. Of whom is Daniel speaking?)

3. According to these verses Christ has all authority. Over what does He have authority?

4. What is one way God is speaking with authority into your life, and what are you doing to walk in obedience to His Word?

Understanding Numbers in the Book of Revelation

John uses a second kind of symbolism in the book of Revelation ... numbers. Sometimes the numbers in Revelation have a literal sense, like the fact that there were seven churches that received this letter. We know this is literal because he lists the churches by name and they were all real churches that existed in John's day. But often the numbers in Revelation are symbolic and it is necessary to get inside what the numbers represent.

For instance, the number seven represented perfection. Because it was the number of days in the week, ancient writers saw it as a symbol of completion and perfection. Another number we find often in Revelation is twelve. In thinking about the number twelve, we need to remember that there were twelve tribes of Israel, twelve judges of Israel, and twelve disciples. The number of twelve and multiples of twelve came to represent the fullness of the people of God—in the Old Testament, Israel; in the New Testament, the church.

One of the most well-known numbers in the Bible is found in the book of Revelation. This number is 666, often referred to as the Mark of the Beast. The Mark of the Beast has to do with opposition to Christ and is to be placed on the forehead and the hand. Where does this idea come from? In Exodus 13:9 Moses gives instructions concerning the teaching of God about the Passover feast: "This observance will be for you like a sign on your hand and a reminder on your forehead that the law of the LORD is to be on your lips. For the LORD brought you out of Egypt with his mighty hand" (Exodus 13:9). Obviously, the people did not wear a feast (or observance) on their head and hands. The point is that the feast day is to be a commitment to God. The sign on their head refers to their thoughts and attitudes. The sign on their hands refers to their activities, the works of their hands. And in saying, "The LORD brought you out of Egypt with his mighty hand" Moses is giving a metaphor for the action of God in delivering the Israelites from the Egyptians, not suggesting it was God's actual hand that brought them out.

Read Revelation 13:11–14:1

5. What contrast do you see between those who have their minds and thought processes marked by Christ and those whose thinking is marked by Satan?

6. What contrast do you see between those who have their hands and actions marked by Christ and those whose actions are marked by Satan?

Read Psalm 46:1−3, 6 and Revelation 6:12−17

7. What do you learn about the power and character of God in these passages?

Understanding Cosmic Events in the Book of Revelation

The psalmist does not mean that the earth actually breaks up and sinks into the sea. What he is saying is that in this world, rulers think they are in control. They think their armies, swords, horses, and armaments will have the last word. But the truth is that, over and above them, God is working out His purposes and human beings will never thwart them! The life of the most powerful human being on the earth hangs by a slender thread that God can snap at any moment. When God speaks, the earth gives way and human beings are seen as powerless before Him.

We also use language like this today. We will say that something "rocks our world" to its foundations. It is interesting to note in Revelation that the catastrophic events that seem frightening and bad to us were generally intended to be a source of confidence to the church. John was writing to a church facing suffering and persecution at the hands of the Romans. What he was saying is that although it may look like the whole world is in the hands of the Roman government and army, one day God will raise His hand and it will all be turned upside down!

8. Imagine you are having a conversation with a seeker who lives with great fear of natural disasters such as earth-quakes and tornados. In light of John's vision of God in Revelation, what might you say to this person?

Understanding Creatures in the Book of Revelation

In our day and age we still use creatures and animals to communicate messages. The use of animals in political cartoons, for instance, is very common. If, after an election, you open the newspaper and see a picture of an elephant crying and a donkey doing a dance in celebration, you know who did well in the election. The animals and the picture they paint tell the story. As long as you understand the pictures and creatures, it makes sense. But someone who has just moved to the United States from another country could look at the same cartoon and have no idea what it means.

In the same way, John uses images to convey things with power, imag-ination, and an exuberant confidence in God. Each of the creatures in Rev-elation helps paint a picture for us of the message God wants to communicate.

Read Revelation 5:4–6

9. What are some of the radical contrasts between the two creatures (animals) in this passage and how do they help us form a fuller picture of Jesus?

10. How have you experienced Jesus as the triumphant Lion of Judah in your life?

How have you experienced Him as the sacrificial Lamb of God?

How can these two images of Christ affect the way you worship?

Celebrating and Being Celebrated

Take time to celebrate Jesus as both the victorious Lion of Judah and the sacrificial Lamb of God. Pray as a group, using these two images of Jesus to guide your praise and adoration.

Loving and Being Loved

God has revealed His love for us by allowing the hands of His only Son to be pierced by nails as He was crucified. Identify one way you can bear the mark of Jesus on your hands by serving Him in the coming week. Take time to evaluate the actions of your hands. Add one new action that honors Christ and commit to stopping one action that is dishonoring to your Savior.

Serving and Being Served

God's Word is like a sharp, two-edged sword. It teaches, instructs, and unveils the plans of heaven. One of the best ways to impact the life of a seeker is to provide a Bible and invite the seeker to begin reading it. Along with providing a copy of the Bible, make yourself available to answer questions and even to join him or her in a regular Bible study.

Consider taking a collection as a small group for the purpose of buying a case of Bibles. Donate the Bibles to your church and request that they be made available to anyone who has a seeker friend who needs a Bible. Your group might even want to take a trip together to a Christian bookstore and look through several Bibles to find one that you feel speaks clearly to those who have no church background. I would suggest looking at *The Journey: New International Version* (Zondervan, 1999), which was developed to help those who are spiritual seekers.

God Is on the Throne

REVELATION 4

There is something fascinating about getting a close look at the inner lives and homes of extraordinary people. Years ago there was a television show called *Lifestyles of the Rich and Famous*. The host took viewers behind locked gates and expensive security systems to see the remarkable homes of people who would probably not call us and give a personal invitation. There was something exciting about getting a look at the lush and opulent palaces and estates of those who live in places about which most of us could only dream.

Back in seventeenth-century France, Louis the XIV built a castle that would overshadow any home featured on *Lifestyles of the Rich and Famous*. He did such lavish work on the castle, called Versailles, that by 1635 there were 36,000 men working day and night shifts on one house! Imagine what your home would look like if you had a work crew of 36,000 men following your every instruction!

In Revelation 4 we get a glimpse of what heaven will look like. What we see is even more incredible than the palace of Versailles

Making the Connection

1. Describe one of the most amazing or fascinating homes you have ever seen. How did you feel when you were in this place?

Knowing and Being Known

The Ultimate Behind-the-Scenes Tour

In one of the most extraordinary passages of Scripture John says, "After this I looked, and there before me was a door standing open in heaven"(Rev. 4:1). John is saying, "I'll take you on a guided tour. You are invited into the throne room of God! I am giving you an all-access pass behind the curtain of eternity." Of course, John is limited to using words, pictures, and images that we can understand to communicate what is far beyond words. This means that part of what we have to do is try to understand the meaning of these images.

John's purpose is to give us a taste of the majesty, wonder, splendor, and awe of the God we serve. The center of this vision is the Almighty God, who is worthy of indescribably extravagant worship. This worship is the unending response of every creature to the beauty, goodness, and glory of the One who occupies the throne.

Read Revelation 4:1–11

(As one of your small group members reads this passage out loud, you might want to close your eyes and try to imagine yourself seeing the same vision John saw.)

2. This vision is meant to wake up our senses. Describe *one* of the following:

    • What do you *see* in this vision?

    • What do you *hear* in this vision?

    • What do you *feel* as you behold this vision?

3. The center of this vision is God Almighty! What do you learn from it about the One who sits on the throne?

Making Your Heart a Throne Room

There are two kinds of people in this world: people who love to get up in the morning and people who do not like people who love to get up in the morning. Some say, "Good morning, Lord." Others say, "Good Lord—morning!"

When you first wake up, what do you carry in your heart? Joy, excitement, eager anticipation? Or worry, fear, and impatience? Maybe the deepest desire of your heart when you first wake up is a longing to get to the closest coffee shop.

What if your first thought was, "God, I know you will carry me in your heart today!" What if that was followed by the second thought, "God, I will carry you in my heart today." Imagine how this focus could transform the rest of your day!

4. How does this picture of God compare with other images of God you have been taught? (Father, Friend, Forgiver, Savior, etc.)

5. What are some of the things you can do first thing in the morning to get your heart focused on the One who is on the throne?

Read Revelation 4:1–3

6. Imagine you are reading this passage to a group of kindergarteners and you have to explain what each image means. What would you say to teach them about the One who is on the throne?

A Majestic and Faithful God

John tells us that he heard trumpets and saw the very throne room of God almighty! The Bible tells us that God dwells in unapproachable light and the vision John records for us is a picture of blinding glory and power. The only words John could grasp for to describe what he saw were precious stones like jasper, carnelian, and emeralds. It was as if the majesty and power of God was illuminating the whole scene.

In this vision John saw a rainbow that looked like an emerald surrounding the throne of God. What Old Testament character do you think of when you hear about a rainbow? Many of the people in those days would have thought of Noah because a rainbow was the sign that God gave to Noah as a guarantee of His promise. We can only imagine what Noah went through after the world was judged by God. What thoughts would have raced through Noah's mind the next time storm clouds filled the sky? "What's going to happen next? Will I come under judgment? Will I be lost after all?"

The rainbow is about God's commitment to be a faithful God. God understands our human fears and insecurities. He let Noah know that the rainbow would be a sign of a covenant, an agreement, between God and His people. From that day on, God would be the God of the rainbow. The God who makes covenants. The rainbow is a reminder that God is the first promise keeper! He is majestic and powerful. He is also trustworthy, worthy, and faithful ... what a combination! When we trust God's faithfulness and behold His majesty our hearts become a throne room of worship.

7. How does the picture of the throne room communicate the character of God?

What is one area of your life where you are struggling today and need to see a vision of the God who is majestic and faithful?

The Power of God

The number seven is often used by John as an expression of completeness. When John writes about the seven spirits of God, he is talking about the utter completeness, sufficiency, and power of the Spirit. In front of the throne there is something like a sea of glass, like crystal. This sea is commonly interpreted as representing the majestic transcendence of God. The throne itself stands in the center of the vision and is exploding with flashes of lightning and peals of thunder. The overall picture is one of sheer power, the omnipotence of God. If we are to make our hearts a throne room, then we must acknowledge God's power. When we carry Him in our heart, we say, "God is able to rule nature, to calm storms, to raise up kings, and to transform human hearts. He can certainly rule and reign in my heart!"

Read Revelation 4:4–6

8. Pick one of the images in this passage and reflect on how that particular word-picture gives you insight into the power of God.

9. The imagery in this passage includes the Holy Spirit (v. 5). Why do you think the Holy Spirit is mentioned here?

10. How are you seeing God manifest His power in one of the following:

    • Your home

    • Your church

    • Our world

    How does experiencing God's power help draw you closer to Him as His worshiper?

Unhurried Worship

We think time passes us by. We remember lost opportunities and think, "I'll never be able to achieve what I've dreamed of. I'll never have the kind of marriage or relationships I long to experience." But while time is our enemy in this world, things are never in a hurry in the throne room. The One who sits on the throne is never rushed. God is untouched, unthreatened by time. He holds all of eternity in the palm of His hand and has all of eternity to give to you. In the throne room, we can give God unhurried worship.

Notice also that just before these creatures cry, "Holy, holy, holy," Revelation records that they say this, "Day and night, they never stop." We make our heart a throne room when we offer constant worship to God. It is not easy for us to offer God praise day and night, regardless of our circumstances. But we need to learn that when things are going badly, as well as when things are going well, God deserves our praise.

Read Revelation 4:6–11

11. What can we learn from the words and actions of the worshipers in this passage?

12. Describe your own pace and the condition of your heart leading up to most worship services that you attend.

What can you do to slow your pace and prepare your heart for a rich and Christ-honoring worship experience the next time you gather with God's people?

Celebrating and Being Celebrated

Tell your small group about a time you experienced God's majesty and faithfulness break into your life. Take time to celebrate God's faithfulness in the lives of your small group members by offering prayers of praise for the many ways God has proven that He is still the God of the rainbow.

Loving and Being Loved

One of our greatest acts of love is to make space to worship God. We need to do this on a daily basis, not just once a week at formal worship services. Jesus Himself taught us the greatest of all the commandments, "Love the Lord your God with all your heart and with all your soul and with all your mind"(Matthew 22:37).

Tomorrow morning when you go to work, let your desk, your cubicle, your place on the assembly line, your house become a little throne room. Only you need to know about this. Commit yourself to offering your work as a gift to God. Sacrifice your own comfort and convenience to do your work well. Every once in awhile just stop and say, "God, I'm carrying you in my heart right now and this work is an offering, a sacrifice to you."

When you step into your car, make it a throne room. Make the table where you eat tomorrow a place of worship. At night when your head hits the pillow, spend a minute saying, "God, I love You and I'm grateful You were with me all day. I'm going to sleep in Your care while You are watching over me, and I'll carry You in my heart tomorrow." When you carry God in your heart, every place you go becomes a throne room.

Serving and Being Served

We live in a high-paced, frenzied world. In this study we talked about the value of slowing down and entering into unhurried worship. Take time in the coming week to pray about one way you can serve someone close to you by helping him or her slow down a little. Think specifically about that person's schedule when it comes to his or her time of gathered worship with God's people. If you are a single person with roommates, you might want to cook them breakfast before Sunday services and do the cleanup duties. Let them know that you are doing this so they can slow down and really prepare their hearts to worship and glorify God. If you are married, identify one thing you can do to take some of the load off your spouse before worship. If you live at home with your parents, ask them what you can do to help relieve some of their pre-worship busyness.

The Most Exciting Five Minutes of Your Life

REVELATION 14

Think about it. What were the most exciting five minutes of your life? Look back on your years, as far back as you can. What were the most breathtaking, emotion-producing 300 seconds you have ever experienced?

I think I could make a good case that the first five minutes after birth might be the most exciting five minutes of life. After nine months of darkness and isolation you find there is a whole world out there full of colors, tastes, sounds, sensations, and lots of other people! If you could remember those first five minutes in vivid detail, you would no doubt tell of discovering a realm beyond your wildest imaginings. If you could have talked at the time and understood what was happening, you would have said something like, "Mom, Dad, I had no idea! I actually had some reservations about leaving the womb, but now I see that this is a much better arrangement. I wouldn't have missed this for anything!"

Although the first five minutes of life out of the womb were a radical and eye-opening experience, it is nothing compared to what we are going to experience the first five minutes after we die! This will truly be the most exciting five minutes we will ever experience. Century after century, many of the brightest minds who have ever lived devoted their whole lifetimes to trying to penetrate what lies beyond that veil of death. Although no one has been able to figure out the answer to the eternal question that puzzles the minds of humankind, God has given us some insight into what lies on the other side.

You and I will experience whatever it is that lies beyond this world. Those first five minutes are coming for each one of us just as surely as the next five minutes will happen as you sit here in this small group. That's reality. As hard as we might try, we will never be able to fully imagine the sights we are going to see, the sounds we will hear, and the experience we will have in those first five incredible minutes of eternity.

Making the Connection

1. None of us can remember our first five minutes out of the womb, and we can only imagine the first five minutes after this life ends. As you look over your life and all the time that lies in between these two events, tell about a time that you remember with great joy and excitement.

Knowing and Being Known

The State of Eternal Blessedness

For some people, the first five minutes of eternity will be the experience of entering a state of blessedness. In Revelation 14:13 we read, "Then I heard a voice from heaven say, 'Write: Blessed are the dead who die in the Lord from now on.'"

In this part of his vision, John talks about seeing a mass of 144,000 people with the Lamb of God. There is some disagreement regarding what this group represents, but I believe it is a symbolic way of talking about all of the people of God. If you remember in session two of this study we looked at how numbers in the book of Revelation are often symbolic. We came to see that twelve represents a full number for humanity (twelve tribes of Israel, the twelve apostles). We also looked at how multiples of twelve have the same sense. The number 144,000 seems to represent the fullness of God's people gathered together before their God.

This one statement turns death upside down. In our world, we think of those who have died as being unfortunate. But John uses the word "blessed" to describe those who have died in Christ having put their trust in Him. He can say this because he knows that they are really alive. In the first five verses of this chapter we get a picture of what this blessed condition looks like.

Read Revelation 14:1–5

2. Imagine yourself as one of these 144,000 who are with the Lamb. What do you see, hear, and feel happening around you?

3. With what you have learned about biblical interpretation in this small group study, choose *one* of the images below and talk about what you think it represents:

    • The name of the Lamb and His Father written on their foreheads

    • The sound of rushing waters, thunder, and the playing of harps

    • The singing of a new song

4. We don't have to wait until heaven to begin experiencing the blessedness that comes from knowing God. How are you experiencing God's blessedness in your life right now?

The State of Eternal Condemnation

It would be wonderful to believe that everyone will experience the state of eternal blessedness John describes in the book of Revelation. However, John's vision gives a very different picture. John says that for some people the first five minutes of eternity will usher them into another reality altogether. The next portion of this vision shows the state of eternal condemnation, an eternal condition best summarized in a simple phrase, "God is not there."

John paints a picture of torment and aloneness that no one would ever want to experience. It is a very different vision than the false notion some people have when they think of hell. I have heard people say things like, "I don't think I would mind hell. All my buddies will be there. At least we will be together." They picture hell like a giant bowling alley where it is always Miller time and they can hang out with their friends forever. That's *not* the picture that John gives. Everything that makes community possible: humility, servanthood, kindness, love, and honesty will not exist in this place. These are all gifts of God, and to reject God is to reject everything that makes community possible.

In John's vision of heaven the images of streets of gold and pearly gates reflect the existence of perfect and eternal community. His picture of hell is the mirror opposite. It is an image of a desolate city just after the explosion of a spiritual nuclear bomb—the end of all community.

Read Revelation 14:6–12

5. What do the various images of judgment in this passage communicate about the eternal condition of those who reject Christ?

42

6. Imagine you could spend just one minute witnessing what happens to those who die and spend eternity in the condition pictured in this passage. How might this change *one* of the following:

    - The way you pray for the people in your life who are not followers of Christ?

    - The way you communicate your faith to others?

    - The way you reach out to seekers who visit your church?

7. What are some of the ways you could respond to a person who tells you they look forward to hell because they want to spend eternity hanging out with their friends?

The Truth Leads to Action

In Revelation 14:6 we read these words: "Then I saw another angel flying in midair, and he had the eternal gospel to proclaim to those who live on the earth—to every nation, tribe, language and people." There is no question that God wants His gospel, the Good New of Jesus Christ, to be communicated to every person we know. Peter reminds us about the heart of the Father for the lost when he writes: "The Lord is not slow in keeping his promise, as some understand slowness. He is patient with you, not wanting anyone to perish, but everyone to come to repentance" (2 Peter 3:9). If God has such a heart for those outside the family, so should we. Since God has made a way through Jesus Christ, we need to hear His call to tell others about the love and salvation He offers through Jesus. Eternity hangs in the balance!

Read Revelation 14:14–20 and Matthew 9:35–38

8. What contrasts do you see between the harvest Jesus describes in Matthew 9:35–38 and the harvest John sees in this passage of Revelation?

9. Tell your small group members about one non-believing person you are praying for and to whom you are seeking to communicate the gospel of Jesus Christ.

How can your small group members pray for you as you seek to develop this relationship and be a witness for Jesus Christ?

10. Talk about what your church does to train people to effectively communicate their faith and consider the following as a small group:

    • If your church offers an effective evangelism training program, encourage all group members who have not been trained in the last eighteen months to take this course together.

- If your church does not offer an evangelism course, have one or two of your small group members agree to meet with your pastor and discuss the possibility of beginning a course to help train church members in personal evangelism. (There are some very practical suggestions for how to do this in the leader's notes.)

Celebrating and Being Celebrated

Take time as a small group to lift up prayers of praise in three distinct directions:

- Praise God for the lives of those who pointed you toward Jesus and who communicated the gospel to you.
- Thank God for those in your congregation who are being fruitful in telling others about Jesus. Pray for them to continue bearing fruit in their evangelistic ministry.
- Celebrate the lives and ministries of the missionaries your church supports. You might want to name a few before you begin praying and identify the part of the world they serve. Praise God for their ministry and pray for them to remain bold as they communicate the love of God revealed in Jesus Christ.

Loving and Being Loved

One of the greatest acts of love you can extend to a person who does not know Jesus is to be ready to communicate your faith in a natural and clear manner. The apostle Peter writes: "But in your hearts set apart Christ as Lord. Always be prepared to give an answer to everyone who asks you to give the reason for the hope that you have. But do this with gentleness and respect . . ." (1 Peter 3:15).

Commit yourself to going through an evangelism training class at least every two years. If your church does not have such a class, help start one. If there is no interest in this kind of training for church members, find another local church that has a commitment to evangelism and take their training class.

Serving and Being Served

Jesus said: "The harvest is plentiful but the workers are few. Ask the Lord of the harvest, therefore, to send out workers into his harvest field" (Matthew 9:37–38).

Serve your local church, the church around the world, and those who are still lost by doing exactly what Jesus teaches in this passage. Commit yourself to regular prayer for God to raise up workers who will go out into the harvest field with the Good News of Jesus. Be sure that each time you pray, you ask God to give you boldness as He sends you out to bear His gospel.

Our Extreme God

REVELATION 19

Over the past few years there has been a new trend toward what is being called "extreme sports." People who have grown bored with sports like skydiving or snow boarding jump out of planes with a snow board strapped to their feet. As they hurl toward earth at unbelievable speeds, they compete to see who can do the most difficult flips and twists as they plummet through the air before they open their chute at the last minute. Athletes who have grown tired of regular mountain climbing have added a new twist to the sport by climbing icebergs or frozen waterfalls with minimal equipment, knowingly facing danger each moment they are on the sheer wall of ice. And the list of extreme sports seems to keep growing each year.

Extreme sports call for serious amounts of risk taking. They are reserved for people who have the sense that life was not meant to be bland or routine, people who want to experience life in all of its pulse-pounding intensity.

Although many of us will never engage in extreme sports, we should all enter the realm of extreme spirituality. We worship a God who is extreme beyond description! In the book of Revelation we see pictures of dramatic extremes: absolute good and pure evil, light and darkness, life and death, heaven and hell. We call this dualism: contrasting images that stand in direct opposition to each other. In Revelation we meet a God who is radical beyond description and who invites us to live on the edge of excitement as we discover extreme faith.

Making the Connection

1. If you could try anything and know you would not be injured or embarrassed, what would you try and why would this be exciting for you?

Knowing and Being Known

Extreme Intimacy

Everyone hungers to be known, celebrated, and loved. This longing started when we were so young that we can't remember a time it was not there. It is so deep that it will never go away.

At the same time, our greatest fear is that we might be rejected or cast out. When a man asks a woman for a date, when he takes a risk and lays his feelings and heart on the line, he fears hearing those four dreadful words: "Let's just be friends." We fear rejection because we long for intimacy. They are two sides of the same coin.

No relationship on the earth, however close and fulfilling, can fully satisfy the hunger of the human heart for intimacy. Only God can meet these deep longings of our heart. One day all of our loneliness and longing will be taken away. In one of the oldest and most beautiful pictures in all of Scripture we read, "For your Maker is your husband—the LORD Almighty is his name—the Holy One of Israel is your Redeemer; he is called the God of all the earth" (Isaiah 54:5).

You and I will experience such extreme intimacy with God that He chose the ultimate image of human closeness to help us understand ... marriage! The highest delight that the most passionate groom feels for the most beloved bride on this earth is just a dim reflection of what it is that God feels for you. The vision God gives John is so intense that the guests see the delight of the groom and the joy of the bride and they can't help but cry out, "Hallelujah!"

Read Revelation 19:1–10

2. What are some of the things that the people in heaven do and say that reveal a deep level of intimacy with God?

3. Imagine a person whose idea of heaven is sitting quietly on a cloud and praying silently. For excitement, they might occasionally play a very gentle harp tune. How does John's vision of heaven in this passage shatter that tame view of what eternity with God will be like?

4. Tell about one of your most extreme spiritual experiences and how it helped you understand God's desire to be in an intimate relationship with you.

Extreme Authority

In our day we have different ways of determining who holds the authority in a given situation. Sometimes it is by the number of bars or stripes on a military uniform. At other times we can tell who has the authority by the size of a person's office or who has the best window view from their desk. But there is one universal indicator that defines who holds the final authority in every home. Simply stated, it is the answer to the question: Who holds the remote? Let's be honest. When you walk into a room with a TV, all you have to do is quickly look around to see who has the remote in their hand, on their lap, or resting next to them. Look no further; you have just discovered who wields authority in that home.

When it comes to this universe, God holds the remote. He has power and authority over every corporation, neighborhood, school, family, and life. He has final authority over loneliness, brokenness, poverty, sin, sickness, the Evil One, and death. Every power will be accountable to Him, including you and me.

Take a look at your life and determine if you are trying to hang onto the reins when God is calling you to bow your knees before Him. Are you hanging onto the remote? Do you have an attitude of bitterness that you need to let go? Are you holding back from serving God or not following Him on some adventure of faith because of fear? If you are, surrender your fear and willingly release the remote control of your life to the One who made you and loves you.

Read Revelation 19:11–16

5. How do you see the extreme authority of God revealed in the images and symbols in this passage?

6. Identify one image in this passage that really strikes a chord in your heart. How can holding onto this image impact the way you obey God's leading in your life?

7. If you were to give God complete authority in *one* of these areas of your life, how might things change in the coming weeks?

- In your professional life

- In your home

- In your free time

- In your use of personal finances

- In your friendships

Extreme Triumph and Judgment

We were made for extreme intimacy with God. Christ has risen from the grave and every day we see His extreme authority in the universe. For followers of Christ, this is good news! But for some people, the power and authority of Jesus Christ is not good news! Those who have rejected the offer of God's love and have rebelled against Jesus' authority will suffer extreme judgment.

At the beginning of Revelation 19 we see a picture of a feast of great joy. Now we see a very different kind of feast. An angel is calling birds to gather for a great supper at which they will eat the flesh of kings, captains, and the mighty. The imagery is very gruesome but it paints a picture of a truth we can't ignore. The same God who longs for intimacy with His children will bring judgment on all who reject His offer of salvation.

Read Revelation 19:17–21

8. What pictures of judgment does John paint? What helps you gain confidence as you read this description of God's victory over evil?

How do you feel when you realize that this judgment will fall on real people?

9. In light of the sobering reality of God's coming judgment on those who don't have faith in Jesus Christ, what can you do as a small group to bear a more clear and extreme witness to your faith in Jesus Christ?

10. What are some of the ways your church does a good job of communicating the message of Christ in a culturally relevant and warmly inviting manner to spiritual seekers?

What are some steps you can take as a church to be more sensitive to those who are not yet in the family of God and let them know that they are welcome at your church?

Celebrating and Being Celebrated

God could have made the world and then stood back like a distant creator who took no personal interest in His creation. Thankfully, He did not! God's desire to be intimate with His children is so extreme that He allowed His own Son to die as a sacrifice for sin so that we could be restored in relationship with Him. Take time as a group to pray a prayer of celebration and praise for God's intimate and amazing love. Pray also for hearts that are prepared to receive more and more of the love your heavenly Father wants to lavish on you.

Loving and Being Loved

In 1 Samuel 15:22 we read, "But Samuel replied: 'Does the LORD delight in burnt offerings and sacrifices as much as in obeying the voice of the LORD? To obey is better than sacrifice, and to heed is better than the fat of rams.'"

Our God has extreme authority over the whole universe. But in His great plan He has decided to give us a choice to yield to His authority or to rebel against it. Take time in the coming week to identify one area in your life in which you are not surrendering to His authority. Confess this sin and ask for the power of the Holy Spirit to fill you as you seek to bring delight to the heart of God.

Serving and Being Served

Identify one way your small group can help make your church a warmer and more inviting place for those who are visiting as spiritual seekers. Take action in the coming weeks to actively work at creating an atmosphere of acceptance and love. If you find this is having a positive impact, encourage other small groups in your church to join in the effort to reach out to those who are reaching out for God.

What Will Heaven Be Like?

REVELATION 21:1–7, 22–27; 22:5

People sometimes wonder what they will do in heaven. It seems that some folks are worried that heaven will be boring. Many people think heaven is going to be like an eternal retirement village.

There are others who wonder about things like, "Will I get to play my favorite sport in heaven?"

There is a story of two friends who had always wondered if there would be baseball in heaven. They both thought that if there wasn't baseball in heaven it just wouldn't be all they could dream of. One day they made an agreement that whichever one of them died and went to heaven first, he would find some way to come back and let the other know if there was baseball in heaven. Sure enough, one of them died, went to heaven, got all the needed information, and came back to give his friend the update. He said, "Well, buddy, I have good news and bad news. The good news is that there is baseball in heaven." His friend was thrilled! He could not imagine what bad news could possibly spoil the moment. His friend continued, "The bad news is that your name is on the roster to pitch in Friday's game!"

Making the Connection

1. When you were a child, what did you imagine heaven would be like?

Knowing and Being Known

In Heaven We Will Be Thoroughly Joyful

One of the very first needs we have as human beings is the need to be comforted. Mothers and fathers begin to give comfort from the first day of their baby's life. When a child is hungry, sick, wet, thirsty, afraid, or in pain, loving parents do all they can to dry that child's tears and make him feel at peace.

Psychologists say that one of the marks of a healthy human being is the capacity to give self-comfort. When our daughter Laura was born, my wife, Nancy, would always say one of two things to her when she was sad or hurt. She would say either, "Honey, honey, honey," or "I know, I know." Those two phrases became ingrained in Laura's little heart and mind. Before she could say almost anything else she learned to say, "Honey, honey, honey, I know, I know." Sometimes she would wake up at night and begin crying. If we didn't get there right away, she would just lay in her crib and say, "Honey, honey, honey, I know, I know." Sometimes Nancy and I would lay in our bed, listen to her comfort herself, and chuckle to ourselves.

Read Revelation 21:1–7

2. This passage reveals a very busy and active God. What do you learn about God in the following areas:

    • What He is doing in this heavenly vision

- What He is saying to His children

- What His character is like

In light of God's character as well as what He is doing and saying in this passage, describe the God we will meet face-to-face when this life ends.

3. What images and pictures in this passage give you a sense of the joy we will experience when we are in heaven?

4. Our God is the same yesterday, today, and forever! We don't have to wait until we get to heaven to experience His joy. Tell about one area of your life in which you are experiencing the joy of the Lord right now.

In Heaven We Will Be Astoundingly Productive

If you remember the story of Adam and Eve in Genesis, then you know we have all been created in God's image. In Paradise, before sin ever entered the world, human beings were called to be productive! We were made to work and be fruitful, to reign in cooperation with God over His creation. After the fall work became painful. But productive, life-giving, meaningful work has always been part of God's vision for us!

The need to contribute is central to who we are, and it will still be part of who we are in the new paradise of heaven. In fact, only in heaven will our gifts and abilities be fully actualized and our need to contribute fully expressed.

In the parable of the talents (Matthew 25:14–30) Jesus teaches that those who have been faithful over a few things in this life will be put in charge of many things in His heavenly kingdom. Some people wonder if there will be intellectual challenges and adventures that require greatness of spirit when they get to heaven. Others wonder if there will be tasks that need strength and will and character. Some wonder if there will be a place for creative, compelling, articulate communication. Of course there will! Dallas Willard puts it like this: "You will know fullness of function, the unending creativity involved in a cosmos-wide cooperative pursuit of a created order that continuously approaches but never reaches the limitless goodness of the triune personality of God." That's what we will be part of in eternity. There is nothing boring about it. We will be amazingly productive.

Read Matthew 25:14–30 and Revelation 22:5

5. In this parable, how does Jesus connect our productivity in this life and our productivity in the life to come?

6. Many people envision heaven as eternal retirement. How do you feel when you think about heaven including fruitful, meaningful, productive labor?

7. Tell about one of the spiritual gifts or abilities you have and how you are developing it and investing it for the Lord.

What can you do in the coming year to sharpen this ability and use it more fruitfully for the Lord?

In Heaven We Will Be Morally Flawless

We all have at least one bad habit. Let's be honest, most of us have more than that! In the gospel of John we read, "This is the verdict: Light has come into the world, but men loved darkness instead of light because their deeds were evil. Everyone who does evil hates the light, and will not come into the light for fear that his deeds will be exposed" (John 3:19–20).

Human beings prefer darkness because of their sin. We can all understand about wanting to hide. There are things we do, and parts of who we are, that we prefer no one else would know. Sometimes we feel as if we are moving in slow motion in our struggle for growth, our battle to overcome sin, and our journey to become the people God wants us to be. Yet we can celebrate the promise that when we see Jesus face-to-face, all this will change. Every moral imperfection will be washed away.

Read Revelation 21:22–27

8. What contrast do you see between the darkness of John 3:19–20 and the eternal light of Revelation 21:22–27?

9. God wants to shine His light on every area of darkness in our lives. He does not want to wait until our life ends, He wants to let His light shine right now. What is one area of darkness in your life where you want to see God shine His light?

How can your small group members pray for you as you seek God's transforming power in this area of your life?

Celebrating and Being Celebrated

Take time as a group to lift up prayers of praise for the inexpressible joy that lies ahead for all who follow Jesus Christ. Pray also that each of your group members would begin experiencing this joy today.

Loving and Being Loved

One day, when we see Jesus face-to-face, we will be made morally flawless. Until then we will all battle with the reality of sin and imperfection. The Bible reminds us that God sees us with all of our moral flaws and loves us anyway. In Romans 5:8 we read, "But God demonstrates his own love for us in this: While we were still sinners, Christ died for us." Take time to identify people in your life who need you to love them, even with their imperfections. Pray for the strength and courage to extend grace and love even when you see their areas of struggle.

Serving and Being Served

God says that work can and should be a blessing in our lives. Take time in the coming days to think and pray about your attitude toward your work. (This could be work in the marketplace or in the home.) Pray for God to give you a new, joy-filled perspective. Pray that you would have the heart of a servant in your workplace and that others would see Christ in you.

Session One — Why Study the Book of Revelation?
REVELATION 1:1–8

Questions 1–4

Why study Revelation? Why work our way through a book in the Bible that takes so much care and energy to figure out? Why not just stick with the portions of the Bible that are easy to read and understand? There are lots of reasons, but one big reason is that it will sharpen our ability to study the rest of Scripture.

By studying this book, you will learn more about how to dig into the Bible and do in-depth, Christ-honoring interpretation of God's Word. The technical term for biblical interpretation is hermeneutics. The concept behind hermeneutics is that whenever communication takes place, there is always a gap between the sender and the receiver. And that gap between the speaker and listener often causes the message to be misunderstood. We have all experienced this in some shape or form at some time in our lives.

In this small group study we will seek to bridge this communication gap and offer tools for interpretation you can use as you study the book of Revelation as well as other portions of the Bible. While we can't look at every chapter of Revelation in a six-session study, we can focus in on some of the key themes. From there you can read on your own and really dig into the text of this powerful book of the Bible.

Questions 5–6

We live in a day and age where versions of the Bible and Bible study tools are plentiful in a way they have never been in history. Many homes have not only one copy of the Bible but multiple copies. We have study Bibles, devotional Bibles, children's

Bibles, Bibles for teens, and many more! While we should celebrate this provision of God's Word in so many easy-to-use formats, owning a Bible and knowing the Bible are two different things. We need to commit ourselves to studying the whole council of God. Every word of the Bible, from Genesis to Revelation, is inspired by God and needful for us to grow into maturity as His followers. We need to identify the areas of the Bible about which we know the least and take time to focus on learning those portions of God's Word. What is your weak link? Is it the Prophets? Psalms or Proverbs? The Gospels? Take time to identify where you need to grow the most in your knowledge of God's Word and commit to learning and following the teaching of this portion of the Bible with all your heart!

Questions 7–9

We can't read the book of Revelation without being confronted by the hard reality that all human beings are headed toward heaven or hell. This reality should lead us to celebrate when someone comes to faith in Jesus. It should also move us to prayer and action on behalf of those who do not yet know Jesus Christ. The book of Revelation gives us a view behind the veil of eternity and reminds us of the sobering truth that a person's relationship with Jesus, the sacrificial Lamb of God, is the one determining factor for where we will spend eternity. We must sink this truth deep into our hearts and allow it to impact the way we live our lives. We must also focus on the identity of Christ. After all, John's revelation is the revelation of Jesus Christ. Christ's identity is central to the book.

Questions 10–11

John was suffering for the gospel when He was given this revelation. The first recipients of the words of this prophecy, the members of the seven churches, were facing intense persecution. Some of them were even being martyred for their faith. Read these words closely: "I know your afflictions and your poverty—yet you are rich! I know the slander of those who say they are Jews and are not, but are a synagogue of Satan. Do not be afraid of what you are about to suffer. I tell you, the devil will put some of you in prison to test you, and you will suffer persecution for ten days. Be faithful, even to the point of death, and I will give you the crown of life" (Revelation 2:9–10).

The apostle Paul knew what it was like to face regular suffering and persecution for the gospel (2 Corinthians 11:21–29). Jesus Himself was persecuted, falsely accused, and crucified when He had done no wrong. The Bible is clear that all who seek to follow Jesus will have times of trials and suffering. Yet in all of this, we can discover that true blessedness comes not in our circumstances but in our Savior.

Session Two — Understanding the Images and Language of Revelation
REVELATION 1:12–20

As we study Revelation, we find that there are four primary kinds of imagery (objects, numbers, cosmic events, and creatures) that are often used as symbols of a deeper meaning. In seeking to understand Revelation, we must begin to ask what John meant when he used these images. It is important to realize that we *can* understand the book of Revelation. It is knowable, and God desires for us to understand the truth He is revealing in this book of the Bible.

Questions 2–4

When we see the image of Jesus with a sword coming from His mouth, we must ask ourselves whose words we are going to allow to have power and authority in our lives.

What happens when your boss begins to speak harsh words to you and you find yourself becoming negative? What if your job is at stake? Does your boss hold the sword in your life? What if your parents inflict pain on you, or your spouse's words are no longer complimentary and loving and finally she says, "I don't love you!" Does your spouse hold the sword in your life? What if your children have moved away and they no longer call you? Who holds the sword in your life when it comes to their words? Whose words have authority in your life?

In Jesus Christ we have someone whose word is absolutely authoritative. Once when He was out in a boat with His disciples there was a terrible storm. Jesus simply looked at the sea and said, "Quiet down! Be still!" And it did! His disciples' response was one of awe and wonder that even the wind and the waves would obey Him. Jesus' words reign over creation, over history, over rulers! No one else's words should be allowed to wield the sword over us—not our boss, spouse, parents, friends, anyone!

Questions 5–6

John is helping us see that those who follow the devil will have their lives marked by the evil he brings. Their minds and entire thought processes will be marked by his way of thinking and their hands will be guided by his will.

The image of the mark on the head and hands of people should not seem that foreign to us. We still use imagery and metaphor like this today. When someone says, "Put on your thinking caps," we don't expect them to actually put on a hat. We want them to tune their minds in and focus because it's time to learn! When someone says that they need to get their "head on straight," we know that it has nothing to do with their neck and spinal column. It means they need to start thinking right. The language John is using is far more about the power of the enemy in guiding our thinking and actions than it is about being stamped with a literal number.

John uses language that would have made sense in his day. Much in the book of Revelation points back to truth God revealed in the Old Testament. Of the 404 verses in the book of Revelation, there are over 500 references to Old Testament imagery. If we find ourselves not understanding much of the book of Revelation, it might be that we are not very familiar with the Old Testament.

In Revelation, when John talks about the mark of the beast, he is referring to those who are opposed to Christ in their thoughts and actions; those who are hostile, proud, and judgmental toward God. In our day, supposed Bible scholars are saying that the mark of the beast has to do with microchips, computer scanners, bar codes, and secret sinister conspiracies of high technology. These things trivialize the message of Scripture. One well-known author claims that the mark of the beast has to do with Visa cards. He says that the VI in visa is the

Roman numeral for six, the S stands for *sigma*, the sixth letter in the Greek alphabet, and the A is connected to the Babylonian number for six. I don't know a lot about the Babylonian alphabet, but I do know that *sigma* is the eighteenth letter of the Greek alphabet (and always has been!), so he is wrong on that level. But the deeper truth is that John is simply addressing the deeper spiritual reality of a battle between good and evil that has gone on since the Fall and still goes on in our world. It rages in my heart and yours! John's passionate desire is for the little flock of seven churches in his day to live in a way that shows the mark of God on their thoughts and actions.

Questions 9–10

In verse 5 of this passage John speaks of the Lion of the tribe of Judah. We know that this lion is Jesus. What a great image for Christ! It is the image C. S. Lewis uses in the *Chronicles of Narnia* as he introduces us to the great Aslan. Just think of Jesus' strength, majesty, and power! Then ask yourself how the Lion conquered. Did he do it with power to overcome his enemies? No! In verse 6 it says, "Then I saw a Lamb." John speaks about a lamb that was slain, which would have been a bloody scene. The Lamb, Jesus, has laid down His own life for us. This imagery sends our minds back to the Old Testament Passover lamb that was slain on behalf of the sins of the people. John looks at the One who was slain for us and he sees the One we love covered with blood. What a powerful reminder of the price God paid for our salvation.

Session Three — God Is on the Throne
REVELATION 4

Questions 2–3

I remember the day we took our son to a theme park for a birthday celebration. It rained the day we went, and for about the first hour and a half he and I walked around the park getting soaked. All I could think about was how wet I was getting, but my son had a whole different perspective on the situation. He noticed that because of the weather very few people had come to the park. This particular park has what is billed as the most nausea-inducing roller coaster in the country. Because there were so few people, there were no lines. My son went on that roller coaster fifteen times! As he stood there with the rain pouring down on him, he said to me, "I picked the greatest day in the world to come, didn't I!" For him, it was enough just to be in the park and ride the rides. He didn't need sunshine or great weather.

As we read Revelation, we also see sincere fulfillment of desire in the apostle John. In isolation on an island, under lock and key, he didn't know if he would ever see his friends again. But for him, it was enough to be in the throne room, the presence of God.

We need to ask ourselves if we can worship God even when things go wrong. When the car breaks down, the kids are fighting, an unexpected bill comes, somebody lets you down, or you're disappointed or saddened, can you still celebrate the reality that God is on the throne? In the midst of a busy and frenzied day, can you still whisper, "Holy, holy, holy," offering up ceaseless praise?

John recorded this vision with a very serious purpose in mind. He was writing to churches facing problems, threats, persecution, and martyrdom. God wants us to know that when we have problems, when we suffer, when we are afraid, and when we are tempted to give up, our heart and life must become a kind of throne room. We need to open our eyes and see the One who is seated on the throne. Because this world often seems random, chaotic, and catastrophic, we need to be reminded that the One on the throne is still Lord over all! He reigns, and the day is coming when His reign will be unchallenged.

Questions 4–5

The One seated on the throne is God Almighty. As a sign of reverence toward God, it was common practice in Jewish tradition to avoid saying or writing the name of God too casually. It is interesting to note in this passage that God is described as having "the appearance of jasper and carnelian." These are two of the stones mentioned in Exodus 28 (NRSV) as being from the breastplate that was part of a priest's uniform. When the High Priest was going to go into the Holy of Holies, he had to wear a very specific uniform. One part of this uniform was a breast-plate that contained twelve stones (one for each of the twelve tribes of Israel) and the twelve names of the tribes of Israel. The first stone was carnelian and the last was jasper, and they represented the whole people of Israel—a fact that every Jew would have recognized.

In Exodus 28 we read that whenever Aaron entered the Holy Place he would bear the names of the children of Israel over his heart as a continual memorial before the Lord. Now in the book of Revelation we learn that God carries the names of His children over His heart. What a beautiful picture! Our names are written in the heart of God throughout all eternity. When we come to Him in worship we know that He holds us in His heart and we say back to Him, "God, I will carry You always in my heart."

Questions 6–7

God's many promises throughout the Bible were often accompanied by a sign as a reminder to us of His promise to be faithful. He gave the rainbow as a symbol of His promise to Noah. He gave the symbol of circumcision as a sign of the covenant He made with Abraham when He promised to be the Father of a great people. Later God made a new covenant, another promise. When Jesus was sitting around the table, after looking at the friends He loved, He said, "This cup is the new covenant in my blood; do this, whenever you drink it, in remembrance of me" (1 Corinthians 11:25). This image of a rainbow in John's vision would have been a clear reminder of God's faithfulness to His people.

Questions 8–9

To whom do you attribute power? Before whom do you tremble? If God is your friend, why would you tremble before anyone else?

The next time your boss is away, sneak into his office. Take a good look at his chair and see if there is any lightning or thunder coming out of it. If there isn't, stop being afraid. You see, there is only one chair in all the universe that explodes with lightning and resounds with thunder, and there is only One who occupies it!

God holds all power in His hand, and if He is your friend He says you have nothing to fear. When you acknowledge, trust, and live in the power of God, you make your heart a throne room. Then God gives you a little of His power, a little thunder and lightning of your own. What we need to do is use the power and authority God bestows on us for His purposes and glory.

Questions 11–12

John uses a great deal of imagery in this passage. There are several ideas about who these creatures are. Incidentally, these are the same characters that are spoken of in the first chapter of Ezekiel. In chapter 10, Ezekiel referred to them as cherubim, which is plural for cherub.

Most likely these creatures are pictured as winged because God is able to act or to send His messengers to act without delay, with swiftness, and with unimpeded authority. They are full of eyes, in front, in back, and all around. That's kind of a gruesome image when you stop to think about what it would look like, but to put it in contemporary language, it's the same thing as suggesting that moms seem to "have eyes in the back of their heads"! It's simply a way of saying that moms just always seem to know what's going on. In this passage, the eyes are most likely an image revealing the omniscience of God that guides the messengers He sends. Nothing confuses Him or escapes His notice.

Session Four—The Most Exciting Five Minutes of Your Life
REVELATION 14

Questions 2–4

What do we learn as we look at these people? First, the Father's name is written on their foreheads. This is in contrast to or opposite of the mark of the beast. In Exodus 13 we learn that the Feast of the Passover, the remembrance of God's goodness to His people, should be a mark on the foreheads of the people: "And it will be like a sign on your hand and a symbol on your forehead that the LORD brought us out of Egypt with his mighty hand" (Exodus 13:16). This does not mean a literal mark of the Passover was made on the skin of their foreheads; rather, it was a spiritual mark. In Revelation, John is referring to knowing what marks the heart, mind, and soul of a follower of Christ. In John's day, a name had to do with a person's character. When we have the name of God on our forehead, our thoughts and attitudes more and more reflect the character of the Father.

In this life we strive daily to live with the name of God written on our foreheads. We long for all we think and do to conform to God's perfect will. But when this life ends and we enter the first five minutes of eternity, all who follow Jesus will find a name written on their forehead that can never be taken away. All negative thoughts and patterns that have cluttered our minds in this life will be gone and our minds will be pure. During those first five minutes, for the first time in our existence, we will think only the wonderful kind of thoughts that Jesus would think. What a blessed moment that will be!

Next the sounds of heaven begin to kick in. John hears the roar of rushing waters and loud peals of thunder. What is this all about? Well, thunder or rushing waters are sounds of great strength. In this state of blessedness we will hear a voice of great power. John also hears harpists playing their instruments. The harp refers to beauty. What John is getting at is that those who are blessed will fully experience the power and beauty of God. We will hear His voice—the same voice that said, "Let there be light," and there was; the same voice that called to Moses from a burning bush; the same voice that spoke to Samuel when he was just a boy; the same voice that calmed the waves and stilled the storm. That same voice is going to speak to us, saying, "Well done, good and faithful servant."

Then John says that the blessed are so overwhelmed that they sing a new song. We will experience God so fully that we must respond. Being in His presence will be such a glorious experience that it will fill us up to overflowing with praise! We don't know the words yet, but in those first five minutes we will learn a song of praise like we have never dreamed or imagined.

In those first five minutes we will know the One who has loved us before time began. In this intimate knowing, God will create such healing and joy in us that no human words can fully express. That, my friends, will be the most exciting five minutes of our lives.

John tells us that these people are, "those who did not defile themselves with women, for they kept themselves pure" (Revelation 14:4). Some people in the early centuries took this to be an indication that God's plan for all who want to live in purity is celibacy. In their thinking, those who had sexual experiences, even in marriage, are less holy. I don't believe that is the meaning here. The point is not that God disapproves of sex. As a matter of fact, throughout the Bible human sexuality between a man and woman in the covenant relationship of marriage is celebrated as part of God's "very good" plan! I believe that John is getting at something very different here. All through the Old Testament idolatry was seen as unfaithfulness to God. It was often referred to as adultery or pictured as sexual promiscuity. When John talks about the purity of the blessed, he is talking about their absolute faithfulness to God.

Questions 5–7

Those who enter the state of eternal condemnation are so locked up in their own pride and self-centeredness that they become utterly incapable of authentic relationships. We have all met people who are so consumed with themselves that they gradually become isolated. Carry that life trajectory to its ultimate conclusion and you will find eternal aloneness.

Imagine being so locked up in the sin of self-consumption that you can never know the joy of friendship, the goodness of serving and being served, the embrace of a loving heart. In verse 11 John says, "And the smoke of their torment rises for ever and ever." Utter aloneness. No God. No community.

In verse 10 we read: " . . . he, too, will drink of the wine of God's fury, which has been poured full strength into the cup of his wrath. He will be tormented with burning sulfur in the presence of the holy angels and of the Lamb." Normally in John's day when wine was poured it was mixed with water. Unmixed wine was quite rare and extremely strong. That's the image John is using here. It is a very sobering one. God's wrath will be poured out unmixed, undiluted, in the cup of His anger.

Many people today are troubled by the thought of God being angry. That includes people both outside and inside the church. They say things like, "My God is a God of love, not a God of anger." The problem is, they are not talking about the God of the Bible.

What we need to realize is that God's anger and human anger are very different. Often when people think about God being angry, we project on Him the worst characteristics of human anger. But that is not accurate. God's anger is no temper tantrum. God is never out of control. He does not experience unpredictable rage, nor is He vindictive or cruel. But the Bible does teach that God has real feelings, including anger. God's anger reveals the seriousness with which He takes sin. When God sees sin, He does something about it. And when this life ends, those who still have sin to answer for will see the anger of God. The good news is that there is a way to have all of our sin washed away. That way is Jesus.

When John sees a picture of fire, sulfur, and the smoke of torment going up for ever and ever, I believe he is using physical imagery to describe a spiritual reality. This image of smoke going up is used a number of times in the Old Testament when picturing a conquered city that has been burned to the ground (e.g., Isaiah 34:9–10). As we look on we are suppose to think, "Once there were homes and schools here, children playing, people who loved each other and cared for each other, and now all of that is gone up in smoke! John uses this picture to create an understanding of the complete loss of community and the pain felt as people are eternally separated from it.

The last word-picture John refers to in this passage regards the concept of no rest. If you have ever been around small children, you know the two times of the day they like the least— nap time and bedtime. Most children hate it. But somewhere along the way between childhood and adulthood, rest becomes a wonderful thing. God Himself worked and rested on the seventh day. He gives us the Sabbath. He gives us the evening for sleep. Jesus said, "Come to me, all you who are weary and burdened, and I will give you rest" (Matthew 11:28).

Rest is about renewal and being delivered from the curse of work. Rest, recreation, and renewal are gifts from God. Those who cut themselves off from God cut themselves off from all hope of renewal. Another way of putting it is that these people get no relief, no rest from a guilty conscience, no break from isolation. Those who will enter a state of eternal condemnation will have no rest from self-centeredness, boredom, self-loathing, regret, resentment, sadness, or the misery of sin. No rest, day or night. And those who are blessed will experience the mirror opposite—they will be praising God day and night.

Questions 8–10

The first part of this passage, verses 14–16, deals with the harvest of grain. This is the harvest of the righteous, the blessed. The second harvest is the harvest of grapes, a terrible harvest of those opposed to God. This passage opens our eyes to the stark reality that one day there will be a harvest in which some will be gathered into the arms of a loving Savior, while others will be gathered and cast away forever. This should wake us up to the need to get into the action and share the love of Jesus with those who are spiritual seekers.

If your church does not have a training program to help people learn how to get out in the harvest field and share their faith, consider starting one. I would suggest that one of your small group members review the "Becoming a Contagious Christian" materials (Zondervan, 1996). The materials include leader's notes, participant guides, and a video to help illustrate how to communicate the message of Christ in a culturally relevant and natural way. Available in an adult version as well as a version for college students and another for high school students, it is one of the most straightforward and user-friendly training programs available to the church today.

Session Five – Our Extreme God
REVELATION 19

We were made for extreme closeness with God. Extreme love. Extreme joy. Extreme meaning. But if we reject God, if we oppose Him, then the Bible says we will end up extremely alone and hopeless. As fallen human beings we have a tendency to drift through life without taking these spiritual realities very seriously. John sharpens the tension in our lives over these issues.

Questions 2–4

John uses the image of marriage to help us understand the level of intimacy God wants to have with us. Allow yourself to enter into the drama. The wedding of the Lamb has come. The bride has made herself ready. Blessed are those who are invited to the marriage supper of the Lamb! And then we read this wonderful line from verse 7, "For the wedding of the Lamb has come, and his bride has made herself ready."

Just think about that. The bride has made herself ready. Most men have no idea how elaborate this process is. There are whole magazines devoted to helping brides get themselves ready! John, however, is talking not about physical readiness but about spiritual readiness. He tells us that it has been granted for the bride to be clothed with "fine linen, bright and clean." This stands for the righteous acts of servanthood and love that flow among the family of God and between us and the world that help prepare us to meet the groom.

Each time we give sincere and authentic affirmation to someone, the bride is more ready to meet the groom. When we slip into the pattern of habitual criticism, the bride becomes less ready to meet the groom. Each time we speak words of love, the bride is more ready. When we harbor resentment and bitterness, the bride becomes less ready. When we take a step toward forgiveness, when we humble ourselves and put aside our own advancement and position and see the well-being of somebody else, the bride gets a little more ready. Each day, we must each ask ourselves what we need to do to become a little more ready to meet the groom.

Questions 5–7

When Jesus rode into Jerusalem on Palm Sunday, He rode in on a donkey. In Jesus' day the horse was a military animal, while the donkey was not. Jesus was sending a real clear signal on

Palm Sunday that anyone who was looking for a Messiah to come and make war had better be ready to be disappointed. He was going to a cross. This passage, however, is filled with images of extreme authority. The image of Christ has changed from a groom to a warrior. This time He comes on a white horse, what a Roman general would ride on after a victory in battle. John wants us to know that the day is coming when all opposition to God will cease.

Another image we find here is that there are many crowns on Jesus' head. In that day, as in our day, a crown was an indication of authority. The fact that Jesus is wearing many crowns shows His extreme authority over every nation and in every sphere of life. Powerful earthly authorities often think they are accountable to no one. With this image, John is saying that the day is coming when all will be under Christ and He alone will hold all authority.

Questions 8–10

There is a reason John uses such extreme imagery here. Do you ever tire of evil that seems to go unchecked and unpunished in our world? Do you ever get overwhelmed when you read the newspaper or watch television? Evil is a very real thing to John and to the people to whom he writes. In this passage he is saying that the day will come when all evil will be judged and totally destroyed by God.

This is something else we should notice about the power of God: the judgment of God prevails without God having to struggle at all. John spent quite a bit of time painting a vivid portrait of the forces opposed to God. The beast and the false prophet in this passage most likely represent the Roman Empire that was terrorizing Christians in John's day. Then John shows us God Himself and His army, arrayed in fine linen. You would think after all of this there would be a long description of the war between God and the forces of evil, but that is not the case. The sword (the Word) that comes from the mouth of the one on the horse (God) is all He needs to conquer. With His Word fire comes down from heaven and consumes the enemy. God does not have to go to the wall or summon up His last ounce of power in the hope of just barely overcoming the opposition. God's judgment cannot be opposed. In the end, evil will be utterly, finally, completely destroyed.

You and I would be under that judgment too, except for the fact that the Lamb was slain. It is only because of Christ that we are invited to go from extreme judgment to extreme intimacy. Richard Foster writes about a dad who was in a store shopping with his two-year-old son. The little boy was having a very bad day. He was cranky and whining and crying, and no matter what his dad did he could not get his son to stop. In desperation the father began to sing. It was kind of a strange song; it was off-key and none of the words rhymed. But as he began to sing, "I love you, son. You make me smile. I like to hear your laugh. I'm glad you're my boy," his son became real quiet and his eyes got real big. He started to relax in his father's arms. When they were done shopping, his dad took him out to the car and put him in his car seat. The little boy lifted up his head, raised his hands, and said, "Sing it to me again, Daddy."

Our heavenly Father comes to us and sings His strange and wonderful song. In spite of all our brokenness and fallenness, He delights in us just as a groom delights in a bride, as a father delights in a son.

Session Six — What Will Heaven Be Like?
REVELATION 21:1–7, 22–27; 22:5

Question 1

What do you think heaven will be like? When people wonder about heaven they usually think in terms of what the living conditions might be or what the environment is going to look like. A lot of people have a mental picture of heaven that looks much like Oz, or Disneyland, or a cloudy world of winged, harp-strumming creatures. Although the book of Revelation gives some insight to what heaven will look like, the real issue is not the environment. Although streets of gold might seem exciting now, they will pale in comparison to the glory of God! What makes heaven is not the carpeting or the wallpaper, it is Who we will be with and what we will become.

Questions 2–4

The day is coming when you will be a thoroughly joyful person down to the marrow of your bones. Revelation 21:4 says, "He will wipe every tear from their eyes. There will be no more death or mourning or crying or pain, for the old order of things has passed away." Paul says that the glory to come is so overwhelming that if we were to put it on a scale, the suffering of this present time would not even register.

Let's get personal. Think for a moment about your deepest hurt. Your worst loss. Your most difficult relationship. The place in your heart that is most breakable. The biblical hope is not that when you become a Christian you get a free pass from the sufferings of this present age. The biblical hope is that you can trust God today, right now. Take your broken heart to Him. Continue to obey Him. Keep trusting Him day after day, because one day God Himself is going to look you in the eye and wipe away every tear.

God will hold you as His son or daughter and say, "Honey, honey, honey, I know, I know." I don't know exactly how He will do it, but He will make everything right. Every aching heart will be made whole, every emotional wound will be healed, every tear duct will be removed because we will not need them any more. Sadness will be gone, not through denial or ignorance, but because God will set everything right. You will be a thoroughly joyful person for all of eternity.

Questions 5–7

If this concept of productive work in heaven bothers you, take some time to read the Genesis account of God's creation. Let the vivid pictures found in those passages touch your heart and mind. God, who is perfect, was working at creation. He actually took a day off when it was all done. Then, before the Fall, he called His people to care for the land, to name animals, to be fruitful and multiply. Allow the message of Genesis and the picture of the first paradise to aid your understanding of the message of Revelation and the picture of the new paradise.

Questions 8–9

The day is coming when there will be no more darkness (Revelation 21:23). We will not need to hide; our character will be perfected. God will make everything new, and that includes you and me. You will have a new heart that will love effortlessly. You will have a new mind through which only noble and good thoughts will pass. You will have a new mouth that will speak only words of moral beauty and gracious truth.

Revelation 21:6 says, "To him who is thirsty I will give to drink without cost from the spring of the water of life." The day is coming when every desire will be fulfilled. Complete satisfaction of intimacy, significance, community, beauty, and love will all be ours. And the very best part of heaven is that God will be there: "Now the dwelling of God is with men, and he will live with them. They will be his people, and God himself will be with them and be their God" (Revelation 21:3). There will be no need for a temple because God will fill every inch of heaven. We will be home with the Father at last.

WILLOW CREEK
ASSOCIATION®

WILLOW CREEK
RESOURCES

Willow Creek Association
Vision, Training, Resources for Prevailing Churches

This resource was created to serve you and to help you in building a local church that prevails!

Since 1992, the Willow Creek Association (WCA) has been linking like-minded, action-oriented churches with each other and with strategic vision, training, and resources. Now a worldwide network of over 6,400 churches from more than ninety denominations, the WCA works to equip Member Churches and others with the tools needed to build prevailing churches. Our desire is to inspire, equip, and encourage Christian leaders to build biblically functioning churches that reach increasing numbers of unchurched people, not just with innovations from Willow Creek Community Church in South Barrington, Illinois, but from any church in the world that has experienced God-given breakthroughs.

WILLOW CREEK CONFERENCES

Each year, thousands of local church leaders, staff and volunteers—from WCA Member Churches and others—attend one of our conferences or training events. Conferences offered on the Willow Creek campus in South Barrington, Illinois, include:

Prevailing Church Conference: Foundational training for staff and volunteers working to build a prevailing local church.

Prevailing Church Workshops: More than fifty strategic, day-long workshops covering seven topic areas that represent key characteristics of a prevailing church; offered twice each year.

Promiseland Conference: Children's ministries; infant through fifth grade.

Student Ministries Conference: Junior and senior high ministries.

Willow Creek Arts Conference: Vision and training for Christian artists using their gifts in the ministries of local churches.

Leadership Summit: Envisioning and equipping Christians with leadership gifts and responsibilities; broadcast live via satellite to eighteen cities across North America.

Contagious Evangelism Conference: Encouragement and training for churches and church leaders who want to be strategic in reaching lost people for Christ.

Small Groups Conference: Exploring how developing a church *of* small groups can play a vital role in developing authentic Christian community that leads to spiritual transformation.

To find out more about WCA conferences, visit our website at www.willowcreek.com.

PREVAILING CHURCH REGIONAL WORKSHOPS

Each year the WCA team leads several, two-day training events in select cities across the United States. Some twenty day-long workshops are offered in topic areas including leadership, next-generation ministries, small groups, arts and worship, evangelism, spiritual gifts, financial stewardship, and spiritual formation. These events make quality training more accessible and affordable to larger groups of staff and volunteers.

To find out more about Prevailing Church Regional Workshops, visit our website at www.willowcreek.com.

WILLOW CREEK RESOURCES™

Churches can look to Willow Creek Resources™ for a trusted channel of ministry tools in areas of leadership, evangelism, spiritual gifts, small groups, drama, contemporary music, financial stewardship, spiritual transformation, and more. For ordering information, call (800) 570-9812 or visit our website at www.willowcreek.com.

WCA MEMBERSHIP

Membership in the Willow Creek Association as well as attendance at WCA Conferences is for churches, ministries, and leaders who hold to a historic, orthodox understanding of biblical Christianity. The annual church membership fee of $249 provides substantial discounts for your entire team on all conferences and Willow Creek Resources, networking opportunities with other outreach-oriented churches, a bimonthly newsletter, a subscription to the *Defining Moments* monthly audio journal for leaders, and more.

To find out more about WCA membership, visit our website at www.willowcreek.com.

WILLOWNET (WWW.WILLOWCREEK.COM)

This Internet resource service provides access to hundreds of Willow Creek messages, drama scripts, songs, videos, and multimedia ideas. The system allows you to sort through these elements and download them for a fee.

Our website also provides detailed information on the Willow Creek Association, Willow Creek Community Church, WCA membership, conferences, training events, resources, and more.

WILLOWCHARTS.COM (WWW.WILLOWCHARTS.COM)

Designed for local church worship leaders and musicians, WillowCharts.com provides online access to hundreds of music charts and chart components, including choir, orchestral, and horn sections, as well as rehearsal tracks and video streaming of Willow Creek Community Church performances.

THE NET (HTTP://STUDENTMINISTRY.WILLOWCREEK.COM)

The NET is an online training and resource center designed by and for student ministry leaders. It provides an inside look at the structure, vision, and mission of prevailing student ministries from around the world. The NET gives leaders access to complete programming elements, including message outlines, dramas, small group questions, and more. An indispensable resource and networking tool for prevailing student ministry leaders!

CONTACT THE WILLOW CREEK ASSOCIATION

If you have comments or questions, or would like to find out more about WCA events or resources, please contact us:

Willow Creek Association
P.O. Box 3188, Barrington, IL 60011-3188
Phone: (800) 570-9812 or (847) 765-0070
Fax (888) 922-0035 or (847) 765-5046
Web: www.willowcreek.com

Continue building your new community!
New Community Series
Bill Hybels and John Ortberg
with Kevin and Sherry Harney

If you enjoyed this New Community Bible Study Guide, look for these others!.

Exodus: **Journey Toward God**	0-310-22771-2
Parables: **Imagine Life God's Way**	0-310-22881-6
Sermon on the Mount[1]: **Connect with God**	0-310-22884-0
Sermon on the Mount[2]: **Connect with Others**	0-310-22883-2
Acts: **Build Community**	0-310-22770-4
Romans: **Find Freedom**	0-310-22765-8
Philippians: **Run the Race**	0-310-22766-6
Colossians: **Discover the New You**	0-310-22769-0
James: **Live Wisely**	0-310-22767-4
1 Peter: **Stand Strong**	0-310-22773-9
1 John: **Love Each Other**	0-310-22768-2
Revelation: **Experience God's Power**	0-310-22882-4

*Look for New Community at your local Christian bookstore
or by calling 800-727-3480.*

www.willowcreek.org

GRAND RAPIDS, MICHIGAN 49530

w w w . z o n d e r v a n . c o m

Bring your group to a deeper level of interaction!
InterActions Series
Bill Hybels

Help your small-group members help each other develop into fully devoted followers of Christ. InterActions discussion guides ask for a deeper level of sharing, creating lines of accountability between individuals and moving your group into action. Each book presents six thought-provoking sessions specifically designed to build on the dynamics and interplay of small groups.

*Look for Interactions at
your local Christian bookstore.*

WILLOW CREEK

RESOURCES

www.willowcreek.org

ZONDERVAN™

GRAND RAPIDS, MICHIGAN 49530

www.zondervan.com

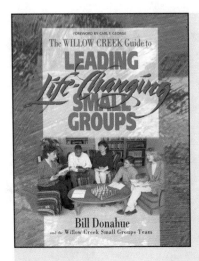

Leading Life-Changing Small Groups
Bill Donahue
and the Willow Creek Small Groups Team

Like nothing else, small groups have the power to change lives. They're the ideal route to discipleship, a place where the rubber of biblical truth meets the road of human relations.

As director of adult education and training at Willow Creek Community Church, Bill Donahue knows that small groups are key to building biblical community and thriving individuals. In *Leading Life-Changing Small Groups*, Donahue and his team share in-depth the practical insights that have made Willow Creek's small group ministry so incredibly effective.

The unique, ready-reference format of *Leading Life-Changing Small Groups*, gives small group leaders, pastors, church leaders, educators, and counselors a commanding grasp of:

- Group formation and values
- Meeting preparation and participation
- Leadership requirements and responsibilities
- Discipleship within the group
- The philosophy and structure of small groups
- Leadership training
- And much more.

From an individual group to an entire small group ministry, *Leading Life-Changing Small Groups* gives you the comprehensive guidance you need to cultivate life-changing small groups . . . and growing, fruitful believers

Look for* Leading Life-Changing Small Groups *at your local Christian bookstore.

Softcover 0-310-20595-6

GRAND RAPIDS, MICHIGAN 49530

www.zondervan.com

We want to hear from you. Please send your comments about this book to us in care of the address below. Thank you.

GRAND RAPIDS, MICHIGAN 49530

www.zondervan.com